First Edition, June 2017

Book cover design: CreateSpace
Illustrations: Createspace

Library of Congress Cataloging-in-Publication Data
Hammad,Duaah
Finding Home/Duaah Hammad
1. Literature and fiction. 2. Poetry 3. Cultural
I.Title.

Paperback ISBN:

978-1=5467076-7-7

Published in the United States of America

1

Table of Content

Chapter 1: An Immigrant's Daughter

3

My life changed the minute I turned three

My mother had spent day and night laying before God

With her palms turned up and a scarf wrapped around her skull

Begging him to give my father a chance in another land

My grandmother always said angels can't bear to see a mother tremble

Maybe that's why soon enough we were saying goodbye to a white and green flag

And looking toward a flag with stars and stripes

I wonder if I had been in their place

Could I have done it?

Could I have left everything I had ever known behind?

All on the string of hope that years later my children would somehow make it?

-There is no bigger sacrifice

4

They did their best to turn a two room apartment into the
heart of Lahore
My mother would welcome my father home every night with
her fingers stained from the spices that reminded him of his
mother
My father would always ask me how my day was
Even when he was on the verge of exhaustion where he
could no longer hear me
All of their paychecks went toward buying my brother and I
new toys
Never letting us feel like things were a bit tight
Every night I would hear stories of the land they left behind
Or I would be handed the phone to talk to a relative whose
face I could no longer recognize
They waited until we were put to bed
To voice the uncertainty of whether we would be able to fit
in here
-They were trying so hard to give us a life on foreign soil

5

The years passed and things only got harder

As I grew older more and more restrictions were placed

I swore up and down I would never be like my parents

Their evasive questions had brought me on the bridge of insanity

The morals they had insisted upon had caused so much controversy

I wanted nothing more but to break free

But the more and more I saw

I realized that this was all because they were so scared of losing their baby girl to the new land

The whispers and expectations of the people back home haunted them

The very thing my mother had prayed to get away from had followed us

I learned that it wasn't their fault that they had such a hard time adjusting to change

There was always another society ready on call to tell them the consequences of changing would cost everything

-Even on the other side of the world there was no such thing as freedom

6

We are so different

Nothing alike but our nose

I remember pushing you away for so long

I would waste no time in telling you that these old traditions

and mindsets don't belong in this country

It took me eighteen years to understand just how wrong I

was

Your under-eye circles came from losing sleep over the

possibilities of what people could say about me

You built us a palace from a few cushions

And lots of laughs

Maybe that curfew you made that I resented all those nights

Ended up saving me the most

Because you knew more than I ever could

-I will never be as strong as my mother

7

I'd like to have met my father

Before the world tried to break him

Could I have a time machine?

Just for a few moments?

To go to a time when he was young and free

Before his attention became driven on protecting his family

When there was more to life than just paying the bills

And putting food on the table

Could I have that time machine please?

Just a few seconds

So I could ask what his dreams were

Did he throw away his own for me?

-The immigrant's daughter would hand over the universe to her father if she could

8

There is not a single soul I adore more than my grandfather

He would stroke his long beard with one hand and the other hand would hold mine as we walked to the playground every day

One day I started playing with a girl who had blue eyes

Her father was too busy flirting with her mother's best friend to notice right away

When he finally looked our way

He stomped over to my grandfather

"Keep your girl away from mine", he snarled

My grandfather looked surprised

"But why?"

"I don't want her by your kind," was the reply

A couple of days later when that man's little girl fell and broke her leg

It was my grandfather who helped her father nurse the wound

-You don't have to wear a cape to be a hero

9

The first time I went to a wedding

I went to first grade excited the next day

My palms covered in swirls of henna

Ready to proudly show them off during recess

The teacher came over to me

She took my hand silently

I could barely keep the smile off my face

Ready to hear her praise

She proceeded to ask why I drew on myself with markers

All the children began laughing

After that

I made sure to scrub my hands raw

For hours

So next time a trace wouldn't be left

-No soap could wash away the pain

10

I was in second grade

When all the children were sent to lunch

I'd dread seeing brown children holding paper bags

The scent of their delicious food would lead other children to
scrunch their nose

One voice would always screech ewwww

And as if it was well rehearsed

Giggles started to be heard

I'd shrink low in my seat

Trembling and praying the ground would swallow me up

So I wouldn't have to see the tear tracks go down that child's
cheeks

-It was as if cruelty was a plague spreading like wildfire

11

I was in third grade when I was called a terrorist for the first time

A small boy turned to me and told me I didn't belong in his country

I reeled back in shock

I tried to explain that I could speak English better than my mother tongue

And that I had shed away traditional clothes for a pair of denim jeans

But he shook his head saying that wasn't enough

I watched as it became a punch line over the years

A quick way to earn a few laughs

I don't think they realized that putting knives into me would have been gentler than the damage their words did to me

Years later I run into the same boy again

I wouldn't have even acknowledged him if he hadn't grabbed my wrist

I braced myself for a taunt

Imagine my surprise when I got an apology instead

That's when I realized it wasn't his fault that he and many others grew up thinking that way

-For a child is not born racist, he is taught

12

There are instances I still see the little girl huddled in the
back of the classroom
Waiting until all the children went out for recess
To let out the tears she had been holding in all morning
The windows next to her were wide open
I could see the sun wishing to cradle and kiss her skin
That was covered in blank ink
From all the notes she had taken on how to fit in
-Sometimes I still see glimpses of the ink when I'm washing
myself in the shower

13

I wish I could have lived in an America pre-9/11

I wish I could have seen what the people had been like

Because now everything is just a mess

It seems that no matter how desperately we try to prove that
we're good

The acts of a few have created a label for my people

That isn't erasable

I just don't want my little brothers and baby cousins to be
scared

Because I know one day on the playground

They will be called that dreaded T word

Just like how I was

-How do you stop the past from repeating itself?

14

I've seen a mosque and a church

I've read the Bible and the Quran both

I've spoken to a pope and an imam

They aren't as different as we presume them to be

No religion encourages the spread of hatred

Its individuals with their own twisted interpretation

That are using fear to destroy everything we hold dear

It's been a decade of defending my faith

Against the accusations and assumptions of the ignorant

-We've grown tired, please understand

15

My aunts weren't wrong for warning my cousins and I
everyday
Careful they said
We're on pins and needles as it is
Do you know what it's like
To feel dread pool into every part of you
Every time you hear there's been an attack?
You have become the home to a volcano
That's too afraid to erupt
Shaking back and forth
You swallow the lava burning in your throat
And begin to mumble back and forth
Please don't let it be a Muslim
-We're still trying to erase the mistakes of others, don't keep
adding to the list

16

Summer of 2016

I watched a racist man spout lie after lie

False claims

And high prejudices

Another ridiculous tweet another day

Everyone thought it was just a silly madman

Six months later

Eyes glued to the polls

You hear a low whimper

And a trembling whisper of "no way"

Turns out the madman turned half the nation mad

His hate went straight from the news into people's homes

-They'll talk about 2017 in all the textbooks

17

You've read all about bad times in textbooks
Watched hundreds of movies on how people were treated
unfairly
But what happens when it's not just a movie but suddenly
it's impacting your life?
A few months after the elections
My vice principal and I stood in the office of my high school
Discussing the possibility of not being let back into the
country if we left for a visit to the motherland
I shook my head arguing there's no way
We're citizens
Sure enough three months later
I'm coming home from my cousin's wedding
And my father and I are stopped as we exit the airplane
All our luggage is opened and checked
-I wonder is it my father's beard or the fact that they can't
pronounce his last name that terrifies them the most

18

Wrapped in my favorite blanket

Laptop screen open for the Skype call

I told my cousins maybe I wouldn't be visiting Pakistan this
year

A frown appeared on my baby cousin's face

"Why does that man hate us"? He asked

I almost fell out of bed

Wondering how such a small child knew so much

He says some Muslims are bad I tried to explain

We trust Allah "Does he trust Allah?" he asked

I held back the tears that were begging to come out

No, no he doesn't

He looked surprised

"Then why are you the one scared?"

-He was only eight

19

Arms wrapped around you as soon as you came into this world
You never knew what it was like to not be loved
But you were warned soon enough that not everyone had your best interest at heart
When you were taught what dresses to wear on special occasions, you were also taught to make sure they weren't too short so you wouldn't attract unwanted attention
When you were taught the differences between right and wrong, you were also taught that many would rather advocate for the wrong than for the right
When you were taught the importance of standing up for yourself, you were also taught that many would love to see you fall
-So many lessons to learn

20

They call to different lands

Asking them to send their people

We'll give them a better life they promise

But then they're so quick to give colored people name tags

They call people with black skin thugs

They call people who are from Latino origin rapists

They call people with brown skin bombers

They're fine with having outsiders doing the jobs that

nobody else is willing to do

-But when it comes time to helping refugees they say there is

no longer any room

In kindergarten we colored drawings of people holding hands around the world

Where you came from didn't get in the way of intertwining fingers

What happened to us since then?

Why did we stop caring?

Is it because schools are being shot up and students are dying?

Is it because the media is dividing us between police officers and black lives matter?

Is it because every time we turn on the news all we see is devastation?

They ask us why we yell and scream in riots

And we show them the blood of our neighbors on the streets

Our brothers and sisters who are no longer in this world

But they don't understand that every death from a different faith is not a win for them but a loss

How can you celebrate what should be mourned

-America, what have you become?

22

I woke up today with my pillow covering my head

My little brother bangs on the door to remind me it's time for school

I throw aside the blanket and reach for my phone

I go on Twitter and first thing I see is the headline

No longer sleepy I read that ninety are dead

And a hundred twenty are injured

I've gotten to the point where the slightest mention of a gun has me distraught

Hearing about shootings have become a weekly routine

And I can't help but wonder

-How long before my own town goes on the list of victims?

\

23

Some nights it all comes crashing down

I see my mother and father watching the news every night

They're careful not to voice their fear

But that doesn't mean I can't see what they're thinking

Or the alarm in their eyes

One night I pass by their room to hear them saying

We weren't safe in the land that we left

And now we aren't safe here

-What will it take to keep our children safe?

24

It's the same nightmare each night

They've found us in the hush of the night

Carefully parking their car in the driveway

They start cleaning their feet on the welcome mat

I swear I can hear their knuckles brush against my door

-I'm so damn scared

25

They say everything comes with age

They tell you that they trust you to drive and not kill anyone as they hand you your license at 16

They hand you a diploma and tell you you're smart enough to live on your own at 18

And by 21 they tell you that you can handle going to a club and having a drink

What age do we have to turn for them to think we're worthy of freedom?

You can't tell me that going to college will solve all 99 of my problems when 98 of my problems exist because of inequality and injustice

You can't tell me that I don't know better when in fact I do

The kids you hushed aren't kids anymore

They're tired of seeing people oppressed

The next generation is rising

-And they promise to do a better job of handing out human rights than the previous generation

26

You've spent nights in different places

Searching behind staircases

Leaving footsteps

And parts of your soul everywhere

Because while you fear what this land could do to you

You've also fallen in love by what it could offer you

So you let yourself grow attached

And devote your time to figuring out how to make it better

Because you know there was a time before these monsters came

And frightened everyone

This land was built on the rights of life, liberty, and the pursuit of happiness

Don't worry, they'll remember that soon enough

I go to sleep every night with the same thought

-Hopefully my children will see a better world than I did

Chapter 2: The Voyage Home

28

Twelve years go by before I returned to the land my parents left behind

When I got off the plane it was like I was in a trance

I stood there in the streets, eyes hungrily trying to drink everything in

Terrified that if I'd look away I'd miss even more than I already had

Time had never been on my side

And I couldn't help but wonder what it would have been like

If I spent my childhood worshipping a green and white flag instead of changing myself for the one with stars and stripes

-The life that could have been

29

When the first trip back home is over you find yourself
sobbing at the airport

Everyone tells you it won't be long until it's time to return

But the tears kept coming

Not at the thought of a departure

But at the image the world had created of your country and
how wrong they were

This was a nation of people done wrong by politicians

Government officials had no remorse that their people were
used to going without power for seven hours

But these people were still so kind and I didn't understand
how it was possible

To be barely making enough to get by

But still welcoming in guests without distress

-Why do you choose to paint them as evil when they're just
genuine poor people?

I wish I could show you the beauty of my homeland

The snow that covers the mountains in Peshawar

The beaches with the never-ending shores in Karachi

The city that never sleeps that calls itself Lahore

A private airport funded by its own people is located in Sialkot

The largest mosque in South Asia lives in Islamabad

My people breathe in the spices that have melted into their fingertips

From spending years perfecting the same recipes

They don't mind spending hours on the threadwork of the scarves that wove around their necks

Taxis are nothing compared to their little green trolleys called rickshaws

The shop vendors never stop ushering you in

Because fashion there changes every week

If you think about it

We're quite similar to them

-Just tired souls with heavy hearts

31

I see how desperately people want to see change

They crave visas as bad as a person who hasn't had a sip of water in days

Their eyes light up when they hear you're from the States

Immediately their tone has changed

They've heard stories of money growing on trees

And acres and acres of opportunity

They imagine it as some sort of fantasy

-You wonder what made you lucky enough to live the American Dream

While you adore most aspects of this land

You find yourself not believing in some of the ethics

When you begin questioning them people shrug their shoulders

And tell you this is how it's always been

There's not much they can do to change it

You try biting your tongue knowing they won't like your response

But after a while of holding it in, you say it anyway

There's not much you can do or you simply don't want to do anything?

-That is the first time they chuckle and say all foreigners think that way

33

The word foreigner had been glued to me like a second skin for as long as I can remember

But hearing the word spit out like its poison doesn't get easier

There are a few who would have never even met me in their minds they still try to paint me as a whore

A characterless girl who parties all night is what they try to make me known for

While knowing that my parents raised me on the same morals they were brought up on

It is automatically assumed that because I live abroad I am not as pure as their daughters

-Because standing up for my liberties make me too modern

34

They reference me as the American

And I didn't mind it

Because it's not like they're lying

What they're saying is true, I do live abroad

I only visit this land once a year

But it was just so silly to me

That the land which gave birth to me first saw me as an American instead of a Pakistani

So how I could blame Americans for seeing me as just a Pakistani when my own country was doing the exact same to me?

-Which country do I please?

35

The war started far before you were born

Men used rifles to knock on your great-

Great grandmother's door

Close your blinds and keep your daughter close they warned

After they left

She turned to her young girls

With a finger to her lips she whispered

They're terrified of our gift

They know our bodies can withstand so much more than their rifles

Never forget my dears

Half of you is titanium

And the other half is gold

-Know your worth

You finally understand where the concept of telling you that everything you are is revolved around what others think came from

I watched them not mind that their sons were out all night

Even as they see the wine glass placed in his hands

And his face is pressed against a female he would have no marital ties too

He is still the apple of their eyes

Yet they'll start calling their daughter after the clock strikes nine

Telling her no girl with shame stays out this late

And if she's seen with any type of boy

Won't matter that he's just a friend

They'll automatically question her character

-These are double standards

37

If a boy notices you

They blame it on the amount of makeup you wear

If he's still staring

They insist it's because of the tight clothes that reveal you

He tries to harm you

And they put a blanket over his sins

Generation after generation they've justified putting handcuffs on their daughter's wrists

And stopped them from being great

Rather than blaming the pigs they've raised

-Please change

38

I wonder do you have a sister?

Surely you have a mother

Or maybe you are the father to a daughter

You call yourself a religious man because you pray five times a day

Forgive me but I must have been asleep

When the Lord gave you the right to question the character of another man's daughter

Would you accept it if the same words you spoke were pointed back at your own daughter?

-Be careful what you preach

We've spent so much time trying to prove to other cultures

that our intentions are pure

Forgetting that as an Ummah we are all divided as well

Is that deed not good enough if it doesn't earn you the praise

of others?

And do you think pointing out someone else's sins makes

you better?

For you claim to be the most religious of them all

But then I don't understand why you spend all your time

judging

And wondering what others are doing

Your concern should be on yourself but it seems

We're all struggling in that field

Religion and culture are not the same

Someone please tell them they've made a deadly

combination

It's worse than every atomic bomb

In the midst of climbing to some spiritual peak

We've forgotten what our religion actually stands for

Someone please tell them

-I've grown tired of yelling

They said sticks and stones could break my bones but words could never hurt me

I was twelve when people told my mother I wouldn't get marriage proposals because I was obese

The numbers came back to mock me each time I stepped on a scale

Holding back my tears

I took their words to heart

Terrified that everyone could hear the wild thumping of my heart

I didn't eat anything but salads for three years

And the strangest thing was

If I starved myself for a few days

They would give my mother compliments the next day

-Children are meant to play with toys not plan how to be the ideal bride

As you enter your last years of adolescence

Hints of marriage come crawling out of the shells and find their way into every single conversation

Your parents tease you

But you can see the pressure is on their shoulders

As vultures come with marriage proposals

I think I was 15 or 16 when the first one came

My mother said don't worry

My father said don't worry

But I still worried

Not for myself but for them

-I knew breaking the system came with a price

42

Arranged marriages still exist

And no it's not like you don't get to see the groom until it's time to say I do

But there is a system that is followed

As a girl you're expected to have a tiny waist and be as pure as an angel when you are placed in front of your future mother-in-law

Her son could have screwed around but the minute she finds out you did

She'll be out the door faster than you can blink

They spend so much time deciding if you're worthy enough to come into their family

As if their honor is the world's greatest gift

-What about my honor, I'm somebody's child too

43

Would you call it a system or a tradition

Of living in a joint family?

And I know it's a great privilege to become part of someone else's family

To be welcomed in not as just someone else's wife but in so many other relations as well

But I'm so terrified of having my life played with on someone else's fingertips

A few sacrifices made quickly turn into a dozen

And a dozen turns into your whole life changed

-I envy white people for being so free

44

I've seen some in-laws

Demand a degree to only have their daughter-in-law sit at home all day making tea

I just can't bear the thought of that happening to me

That all those years I had spent in school memorizing books and all the all nighters I pulled to make sure assignments were turned in on time

Had all just been so I could be on display as someone's trophy wife?

I wonder when it'll be considered good that both a son and daughter work?

-I pray my future daughter has it better

45

My sincerest apologies to every girl who was blamed for rape

The girls who were looked down upon for being divorced

The ones who found love but were shunned

Nationalism is a strong thing

But disowning your child for marrying outside your race is insane

To the girls who have taken years of domestic abuse with no complaints

All for protecting the family name

To the men who claim to be protectors of faith

-This isn't saving honor, this is slaughter

46

There is so much arrogance affiliated with family name

Some put their noses in the air

Holding their heads high

Looking down at all the people walking by

But why?

Why would you want to carry a name

So proudly

That it becomes a burden?

-Why do they try to turn a last name into an identity?

47

There's a belief in the evil eye

"Nazar" is what they call it

I know many think it's just a superstition

But I've seen the damage it leaves behind as it passes

How devastating it is that we shouldn't fear our enemies as much as those who only claim to be our friends

Jealousy erupts from the very bottom of stomachs

And turns eyes green with envy

It's the oldest story in the book

They'll tell you to do well

But they can't stand to see you do better than they are

-When is this all gonna end?

48

Some people spend their days promoting "Nazar"

So they can pick up the phone

To call their friends

And pick apart your flaws

Determined to destroy your character

Just for a bit of fun

But all hell breaks loose

When someone says something about their child

-What goes around, comes around "aunty ji"

49

There is no beast that can stop me from returning to this land

I will do everything I can to make a difference in helping my people

But I know there will be many that will wish to see me fail

Protectors of faith I ask you to put down your weapons

I do not wish to corrupt your daughters

I wish to paint you in such a vision

That the world will never be able to call you evil again

I know this country is worth so much more than what they say

And I will spend the rest of my life proving that to them

-This is the oath to my drowning country: I will save you-- just give me some time

Chapter 3: Shipwreck

51

You were brought over to the new world

Not expecting anything but a warm welcome

Little did you know that acceptance wasn't given on a silver
platter

In the midst of chasing it

-You became your own worst nightmare

52

You craved the approval of children with blue eyes

One day you went to your mother

And asked if you could dye your hair

She hesitated but asked what color

-Platinum blonde please

53

Belonging to two lands became too much at some point

Each flag demanded that I forget the other one exists

It would have been easier to cut myself in half

When did this become a game of who could lay claim?

-And who made me the prize?

54

You were a teenager when you began hating everything

Resenting your parents

Fighting with your uncles

Trying to get away from your aunts

-It seemed like the whole world was against you

55

One day they took you the outskirts of DC

To get your mind off of everything

As you looked around

The sound of a sailboat's whistle made you turn

-It was love at first sight

56

You snuck out that night

And went back to the port

Letting your feet dangle in the water

As your fingertips traced the outside of the boat

-The very beginning

57

You kept returning

Even going as far as taking a boat

There was no fear

Because every time you stepped on that boat

-There was no expectation that could follow you

58

One day your father decides it's time for a break from the West

So we set sail for the East

But you're quick to realize

That while the East and the West are different for hundreds of reasons

-They both specialize in trying to take the best parts of you

59

You keep running between both lands thinking that it's the only option

As you sail away from the East's port they scream traitor

As you sail away from the West's port they scream foreigner

One side says you're too liberal and the other side says you're old fashioned

-I don't even know what I am anymore

60

You've learned the secret on how to keep everyone happy

How to balance living two different lives

Everything is where you can handle it

Until one day someone asks

-Which land are you willing to die for?

61

Everywhere you've visited

People insisted that you needed their permission to breathe

But when they asked which land would you die for

I almost asked if they had an oxygen mask

-That was when the pressure began choking me

62

You made many companions along the way but only a few
stuck around

You realized the rest were just the same lost souls in
different bodies

They knew you were different and that's why they walked
all over your ship

They envied the way the salt water could not make you sink

-Your strongest anchor was your spirit

63

Somewhere along the way

You got lost

Not remembering where you misplaced the map

So you decided to stay put in the middle of the ocean

-It's not like either land wanted you anyway

64

The oceans began crashing against you after some time

It seems your loved ones were able to trace you

They asked the ocean to talk some sense into you

With a solemn expression the ocean promised them

-No harm would come to their treasure

65

I lay awake in my cabin

Listening to the ocean and ship whisper

I toss and turn

All I was good at was causing others to worry

-Drowning seemed like a good option

66

One day after hearing your mother's sobs

The wind decides you've had enough time

They called to the sky

Our little girl's all grown up, shed a few tears would you?

-I wasn't expecting it to pour

67

The raindrops come down the same time the boat gets hit

Lightning chooses that exact moment to strike the middle of the ship

Fate appears in a cloaked gown

He raises one gloved hand and shoves the cloak away from his face

-I drop onto my knees when I realize I'm looking at myself

68

A gloved hand tenderly strokes my face as I shiver uncontrollably

A voice that wasn't my own spoke softly

Why do you carry the weight of the world on your shoulders, my love?

The blood in your heart beats for two countries

-Who said you had to punish yourself for that?

69

My eyes widen through the raindrops

The gloved hand falls away from my face as it goes to pull up its hood again

Your hands scramble to get a hold of fate's gown as he backs away

"Wait does this mean I don't have to pick just one land?" I scream

-But as quickly as he came, he was gone

70

Arms hugging yourself tightly

You heard the waves whisper

You've been sailing and running for so long sweetheart

It's time to stop

-I didn't even realize I was close to the railing until I grasped
it to jump

71

The fall was the most liberating thing

The cold breeze gushed across your face

The salty water coiled itself into vines

Making its way inside your mouth

-It had been waiting ages to taste you

72

You refuse to drown now

After not living for so long

You realize there's still so much to be done

You have yet to claim your home

-Your last breath will be after saying "land ho"

73

You command the air to go back into your lungs

And like an obedient child listening to his mother

He did as he was told

But does you an extra favor by

-Giving parts of you that had been asleep for years a gentle
nudge

74

You turn backwards to see your ship

Gently being pulled down underwater

It waves a final goodbye with a sad smile

I could have sworn I heard a scream

-Years later you realize it was your own

75

In the distance you see a glimpse of land

Of the water being pushed back

Did the salt water get in your eyes

Or are those actually two flags standing on the same side?

-I could feel the warmth of fate's smile

76

The shore had the sweetest smile
As she welcomed me with open arms
She chattered on about how they had been waiting for me
I looked back at where my ship had sunk
-I'm sorry it took me so long

Chapter 4: Land Ho

78

It took a long time

for my palm covered in henna to put aside her fear

And come up beside the palm that was bare

And make love to the idea

-That I had always been enough

79

One night you're putting cream all over your bruises

And you wonder when they'll stop hurting

They tell you the hardest part wouldn't be dealing with the marks

It wasn't possible to come out of a battle without scars

They'd soon heal and only the slightest reminders would be left on your flesh

But what about the reminders that had been imprinted on the inside?

The hardest part would be healing your state of mind

And learning that giving forgiveness isn't up to the angels, in fact it's your call

-Peace will only come if you accept the apologies the universe has been sending

80

What you survived will become part of you

You'll build so many walls around yourself at first

To give yourself reassurance

That the pain won't be able to touch you this time

But understand this

What you survived will stop destroying you

-When you learn that nothing but misery and sorrow will
come from trying to undo what has already been done

81

If there was such a thing as time machines I would give you one

So you would be able to go back in time and protect yourself

But my love

There are none

What I've learned is that we become what we need to be

And sometimes that ends up being what we wanted to be or it's the very thing we swore we would never be

-Everyone has a different survival tactic

82

I didn't think I was capable of sending my tormentors anything but fury

How long did it take us to stop being masters at pretending?

Understanding the ignorant ideology they worshipped was toxic

Let the onlookers know

They will get my mercy

-When they vow to not stand in the way of when I start a revolution that should have started decades ago

83

The first thing I will teach my daughter

Is that being a colored women is one of the greatest but scariest things

Two lands will hand over their demands to you

They will tell you that you aren't beautiful if you don't fit their standards of beauty

They will tell you are obese if you can't fit into a pair of skinny jeans

They will tell you to devote all your time to fulfilling other people's dreams instead of asking

Wait, what are your own dreams?

But don't worry,

The North and South will come to save you like they saved me

You don't have to be your own savior when there are others that would put their lives on the line for you

-After all, you are God's most precious gift

They tell me that this revolution will be good for nothing

I shake my head saying I spent my life fighting useless wars

This is the first thing that has any good reason behind it

They tell me the price of this could be my honor

I tell them my honor has had a bounty price on it since I was born

I've learned how to protect it

But you're not worried about my honor

-You're just scared that the ignorant might actually be found guilty for this one

85

You were far too interesting for them to ignore

They had spent so much time pursuing you

That now they couldn't help but keep tabs on you

They were surprised to be seeing you fly after they told you that you couldn't

They called up your birthplace

And asked them on the phone

Where did she find such a pair of wings?

Pakistan smiled proudly

-The universe gave them to her when she broke free

86

Barbarians brought up to defy humanity

Came to attack my sisters

Like wild animals

Sucking off each layer of their skin

But they forgot

That every beautiful thing is used to being taken advantage
of

One by one

My beloveds

Picked themselves up from the floor

Promising to avenge themselves

-Judgment day will come

Our parents were never scared of the idea of love

They were scared of how we had mistaken it for lust

Your father knew that the boys with cocky smiles

Were just playing with fire

The sparkle in their eyes didn't hide the hint of their desire

The possibility of the chase ending in her baby girl getting engulfed by flames was so troubling to your mother

That she spent her entire existence

Teaching you how to stay away from fire

-I was not raised to be swayed by the sugar-coated words of fools

88

It isn't possible to accomplish everything over night

You start from baby steps

And a little while later it starts to get you somewhere

I've seen my parents slowly come out of the shells that tradition tried imprisoning them in

We don't fight anymore

I mean we still do

But I'm over the phase of trying to fit in

And they've given me more freedom than some of our relatives can tolerate

They've come a long way

That needs to be acknowledged

-The man and woman who got off that plane years ago are not the same

89

I sit in my backyard

With a hot cup of tea

The sun's about to set

When I hear the noise of an airplane about to land

I can imagine that somewhere in the midst of all those people

There is a couple

A woman rubbing her large belly

And a nervous man

Coming here for the exact reasons my parents did

-I ask fate to be gentle with them

90

It's close to graduation when I visit my elementary school teachers

They insist on giving me the tour to see how much I remember

When we enter the cafeteria we begin to pass by tables until the smell of curry stops me in front of a little boy holding a brown paper bag

That smells delicious I tell him

A warm smile thanks me in response

We go to the playground and I see little girls playing hopscotch

I can see henna on one of the girl's hands and when she catches my eye I raise my own hand to show her the patterns on my own hands

She excitingly turns to her friends and points to me and I can't help but laugh when I feel all their eyes on me

And then we make it back to my third grade classroom and I saw that the flag with stars and stripes from my time was still there

We were the two ancient things in the room

-It's nice to you again old friend

91

Every so often men fear the thought of the world ending

And I tell them

For so many the world has already ended countless times

But they find that despite every catastrophe occurring the sky
still prepares to welcome the sun the next morning

-The moon swore that darkness could only accompany you
until the light woke from slumber

92

I'll give you a knife

And I'll grant you permission to cut me open

Stupid right?

Why give an enemy a weapon?

So they can see that despite my skin being a different color

My blood is just as red as theirs

-We're all different in our own ways, but we all bleed the
same way

93

Is it wrong to believe in shooting stars?

Does one truly ever get too old to watch fairytales?

Is it foolish to believe in the man who said he's changed?

Perhaps it is

But despite everything

I will believe in the greater good of mankind

For every bad person that's out there

I'm sure there are ten that are good

I believe the world will begin to heal soon enough

We just need to give it time

To recover from all the destruction we've caused

-A dreamer has hope for the future

94

Nobody plans to die

Nobody plans for war

Nobody plans for the bad things happening

We plan what we're going to wear on our wedding day

We plan what we're going to name our kids

We plan all the good things

-When are we gonna plan to put aside our differences and

accept one another?

95

We're given one life

There are no replay buttons or second chances

So go and make sure you live

Fight for what you believe in

Stop being afraid

Because if you live while not actually living

Regret will come after you years later

And it will do to you things worse than what failure could

have done

-Regret will consume you

There will come a day

When students will spend time studying, hoping to earn a place in Afghanistan's best college

They will beg to visit Bangladesh and touch their beautiful flowers

They will flock to Somalia like birds to get a taste of their culture

Syria's skyscrapers will put New York's to shame

Statistics will say Lebanon has the most tourists visiting

Girls will wish they could have their dream wedding in Sudan

Iran will have adopted fashion week from Paris and play host to the world's prettiest models

People in Iraq will be baffled by the idea of war

And flying PIA will be an honor

-You broke the East with your bombs but they will rise again, that is my promise to you

America has and always will be great

But there seems to be a myth in some parts

That a few aren't as welcome as they used to be

I'm sure there's been some type of mistake

Every black woman

Every Syrian refugee

Every Mexican man

Every Indian girl

Every Korean boy

Every Muslim baby will always be welcomed here

Don't pull out the go back to your country bullshit

This is our country

-Red, white, and blue are the colors of my home

98

To the dreamers

I hope you never stop believing

To the survivors

I hope you find the peace you've been searching for

To the victims

I hope you get justice for what they did

To the romantics

I hope you never fall out love

To the stargazers

I hope the sparks in your eyes never go out

To the children

I hope I live long enough to see the great things you do and become

-Thank you so much for letting me tell my story

99

This is supposed to be the page that talks about the author

But you've just read so many pages about me

You've read all there is to know

Except one last thing

I wouldn't be who I am if it were not for an angel

I was surrounded for a long time by adults who said writing was just a phase

She's the reason you hold this book today

-Asma Ashiq, I love you

Made in the USA
Columbia, SC
04 June 2018